CQRS and Event Sourcing
Master the Powerful Design Patterns

Table of Contents

Chapter 1. Introduction

Dive into the engrossing saga of CQRS and Event Sourcing, two pivotal design patterns, in our special report. The labyrinthine world of software architecture often showcases complex topics, and these two patterns are no exception, poised at the deep end. Fear not, this report intends to unravel their intricacies in a lucid and digestible manner. It's engineered for learners and professionals alike, seeking to master these potent tools. It's not just about theories but also their practical implications and real-world applications. Irrespective of your technical background, this riveting journey will equip you with a clear understanding and empower you to harness the transformative potential of CQRS and Event Sourcing. Brace yourself - we're about to defy complexity and venture into an adventure of knowledge and proficiency.

Chapter 2. Unveiling the Concepts: CQRS and Event Sourcing

There's an aphorism often quoted in software architecture that says if all you have is a hammer, every problem looks like a nail. However, when considering the magnitude and complexity of most software development projects, a single tool – or design pattern – can hardly cover everything. Command Query Responsibility Segregation (CQRS) and Event Sourcing are two complementary patterns that provide advanced solutions for complex architectural problems.

2.1. Understanding the CQRS Pattern

CQRS stands for Command Query Responsibility Segregation. It is a design pattern that separates read and write operations into different models, thus segregating responsibilities. A simplified explanation of the CQRS design pattern might look something like this:

1. Commands are methods in a model that change the state of an object but do not return a response.

2. Queries are methods that return data but do not change the state of an object.

```
public interface Commands
{
    void createOrder(OrderData order);
    void cancelOrder(OrderId orderId);
}
```

```
public interface Queries
{
    OrderData getOrder(OrderId orderId);
    List<OrderData> getAllOrders();
}
```

The separation into commands and queries can provide several benefits. First, it can simplify models by separating the responsibility of reading data from writing data. This makes the codebase easier to maintain and develop further. Also, it can increase performance by enabling separate scaling for read-heavy or write-heavy parts of an application.

In traditional architectures, the same data model is used for read and write operations. This can lead to conflicts when scaling the system, as the needs for reads and writes can be very different. CQRS provides a solution by segregating the two, which leads to more flexible and scalable systems.

2.2. Applications of CQRS

CQRS is often used in systems with high throughput or complexity, where flexible scaling, performance, and data consistency are paramount central. Examples include e-commerce systems, financial applications, and real-time data processing systems.

However, CQRS is not something to apply across an entire system unless the system calls for it due to associated complexity. Instead, it's more suited for specific portions of a system that require the benefits CQRS offers.

2.3. Unfolding the Event Sourcing Pattern

In contrast to CQRS, Event Sourcing is a pattern where state changes are stored as a sequence of events. Instead of updating a state directly, events are recorded detailing how the state should change.

This is not general practice in most systems, where only the latest state of a system is stored and past states are overwritten. This is illustrated in the following pseudo-code:

```
var bankAccount = new BankAccount();
bankAccount.deposit(100);
bankAccount.withdraw(50);
database.save(bankAccount); // Only the latest state
(Balance: 50) is stored
```

With Event Sourcing, each state change would be stored individually. This means the system has a complete history of every event and state change. The latest state can be obtained by replaying every event from the start.

For instance, the above example with Event Sourcing could look something like this:

```
var bankAccount = new BankAccount();
bankAccount.deposit(100); // Event: Deposit of 100
bankAccount.withdraw(50); // Event: Withdrawal of 50
database.saveEvents(bankAccount.getChanges()); // Save
all events
```

2.4. Applications of Event Sourcing

Event Sourcing proves useful when you want to have a detailed historical trail of all state changes made in your system. It's popular in systems with stringent auditing requirements or systems that require complex business intelligence and reporting solutions.

Applications of Event Sourcing include, but are not limited to, finance (where every transaction is critical), complex analytical systems, or debugging (being able to replay scenarios to find bugs).

2.5. Synergy of CQRS and Event Sourcing

Although CQRS and Event Sourcing are two independent patterns, they often play well together. In a CQRS architecture, the command model could use Event Sourcing to store changes, whereas the query model could use state projections for fast read operations. This combination can address the needs of complex, high-load, and data-intensive systems.

In conclusion, CQRS and Event Sourcing are powerful design patterns that are an indispensable part of a software architect's toolbox. They provide solutions to complex architectural problems around data management and state handling, particularly in large, high throughput systems. However, each system has its quirks and complexities, and it's crucial to thoroughly evaluate the system needs before deciding on an architecture and design patterns to use.

Chapter 3. Under the Hood: A Deep Dive into CQRS

In recognizing the architectural patterns acting as antecedents to contemporary software architectures, CQRS, an acronym for Command Query Responsibility Segregation, warrants attention. It marks a depart from the conventional architectural setup where reading and writing operations use the same data model. Instead, it elegantly segues into two distinct models - one for updating data (the command model) and another for querying data (the query model). This bifurcation bestows benefits, including scalability, flexibility, and the ability to mutate data structures independently.

3.1. Understanding the Basics

The CQRS pattern pivots on the principle of segregating operations that read data from operations that write data based on the belief that the design and implementation of each operation should be isolated. This segregation, though similar to the classic database model of CRUD (Create, Read, Update, Delete), transcends it in complexity and flexibility.

Although CRUD appears pristine and competent in simple use-cases, it falters when subjected to complex, transactional operations typically found in enterprise-level applications. This is where CQRS thrives. It posits that the model of an application's commands (write operations) should differ from that of the queries (read operations).

3.2. The Command Side

The command model handles all changes to the application state. They are typically named in the imperative, such as `CreateOrder` or `UpdateUser` and represent an instruction for the system to perform a specific action.

Command operations cannot return data. Instead, they return a status code or void, signifying the operation's successful completion or failure.

Here's a simplistic view of this:

```python
def create_user(user):
    ...
    # Executes some logic, changes state, and returns
    nothing
```

3.3. The Query Side

In contrast, the query model is designed for presenting data to the user. Query operations do not alter the state but extract and return data, often in a highly denormalized, optimized manner for specific views. Here lies the power of CQRS: each view can have its data model optimized for its specific needs.

Consider this example:

```python
def get_user(user_id):
    ...
    # Executes some logic, returns data, and doesn't change
    state.
```

Through such bifurcation, CQRS advocates the creation of simple, specific models over one complex, generalized model that caters to all operations, leading to a clear, purpose-built, and efficient system.

3.4. Stalwarts of CQRS: Advantages

From increased system performance to unhindered flexibility, the merits of embracing the CQRS pattern are as follows:

3.4.1. Scalability

Solitary implementations often suffer from limited scalability due to a single database being tasked with handling both the write-load and the read-load. CQRS circumnavigates this by implementing separate models for the reads and the writes, allocating data handling to different servers. This allows for each model's individual scaling based on the needs of your application.

3.4.2. Simplicity and Flexibility

By isolating the data handling models into two, both can be individually optimized to their specific needs, making them simpler to design, implement, and update. Moreover, this segregation offers you the flexibility to alter data structures, independently adopt distinct data storage technologies for each model, or even rewrite an entire component without affecting the counterpart.

3.5. Common Misconceptions and Cautions

Even though CQRS presents a multitude of benefits, it is not a silver bullet for all architectural problems.

3.5.1. Not a Top-level Architecture

CQRS is a tactical design pattern geared towards specific sections within your system rather than the system's entirety. Thus, attempting to implement CQRS throughout your system is both unnecessary and could become counterproductive by complicating simple use-cases.

3.5.2. Increase in Code Complexity

CQRS inherently increases the codebase size as the implementation of separate models for the reads and the writes is requisite. Additionally, the synchronization between these models can introduce further complexity.

In conclusion, although the implementation of CQRS might initially appear daunting, it proffers undeniable benefits in system scalability, flexibility, and performance, especially in complex, enterprise applications. Bearing in mind the potential for increased code complexity, it mandates a careful, judicious approach in understanding the needs and core use-cases of your application before its adoption. As you proceed in your journey with CQRS, this balanced perspective will hold you in good stead, paving your path to architectural mastery.

Chapter 4. Pillars of CQRS: Commands and Queries

The CQRS pattern, or the Command Query Responsibility Segregation pattern, fundamentally splits an application into two parts: the Command side and the Query side. This section aims at providing a deep understanding of these pillars, bearing the gravity of CQRS.

4.1. The Command Side

In CQRS, the Command side is responsible for all actions which change the state of the system. It can be thought of as the write model. Commands could be anything from placing an order, transferring money from one bank account to another, or updating a user's password.

Often, these commands aren't simply changes in a database. They can also encapsulate complexity like rule validation, logging, or other side effects. For illustration, a PlaceOrder command might need to ensure that a user has enough balance, update respective inventory records, and send a notification to the shipping department.

```
class PlaceOrderCommand {
  constructor(orderId, orderDetails, userId) {
    this.orderId = orderId;
    this.orderDetails = orderDetails;
    this.userId = userId;
  }
}
```

This encapsulation of intentionality in commands not only provides a clear language for discussing system behavior but makes it easier to test the correctness of our applications. It becomes possible to apply the rules of the system to commands and check their outcome without necessarily bringing in the entire modeling domain.

4.2. Event Sourcing in Commands

Commands go hand-in-hand with Event Sourcing. When a command succeeds, it produces events - records of system changes. Instead of recording the updated state, the system records these events. This approach allows the system to 'replay' these events later to derive the current state. Also, it offers excellent prospects for auditing, debugging, and enhances system resilience.

```
class OrderPlacedEvent {
  constructor(orderId, orderDetails, userId) {
    this.orderId = orderId;
    this.orderDetails = orderDetails;
    this.userId = userId;
  }
}
```

While the concept of event sourcing may sound daunting at first, seasoned developers and architects appreciate the flexibility it offers, particularly in systems with complex business rules.

4.3. The Query Side

On the other hand, the Query side of CQRS, as suggested by the name itself, handles queries. This part of the system is responsible for representing the current state and making it available to the clients. It is also known as the read model.

The clients, in this case, could be different user interfaces, or the same system's Command side, or even another system altogether. The query model designs and presents views based on multiple data entities.

For instance, if a user wants to view an order's details, the query model will fetch data from several entities, like Order, User, Item, and Inventory, and present it as a single read model.

```javascript
class OrderDetailsQuery {
  constructor(orderId) {
    this.orderId = orderId;
  }
}
```

The operational independence of the Query side gifts us the flexibility to optimize it for performance and structural adequacy. It's usually a straightforward representation of the data and often denormalized to improve read efficiency.

4.4. Implementation of Command and Query

In a typical modern system, commands and queries have separate data storage systems. Two models can exist in separate databases, use different types of databases (NoSQL vs. SQL), leverage different schemas in the same database, or even live in different microservices.

If a Command operation changes the state of the application, the same change is propagated to the Query model, thereby ensuring data consistency. This synchronization could be synchronous, using something like two-phase commit, or asynchronous, leveraging Domain Events, which make the system more resilient and flexible.

These implementations embrace the principles of CQRS and help us design systems that can scale and evolve. It eases the cognitive load by separating the 'write' complexity from 'read' simplicity and lets us focus on their separate, optimized solutions.

In the vast world of software design patterns, understanding the pillars of CQRS – the Command and Query, lays a solid foundation for venturing deeper. While they appear as mere system operations, their sophisticated segregation offers system designers potent tools to address diverse business demands and complexities.

Chapter 5. Event Sourcing: The Time Machine of Software Architecture

Event sourcing design pattern is an enthralling concept for many developers, evoking a sense of time-travel within software architecture. The pattern unveils a unique approach towards data management, where the state of an object isn't tracked directly, but derived from an ordered series of events.

The conventional method of CRUD operations gives way to a transformative model that traces the state of an object from its origin to the current moment. While the pattern may seem challenging initially, with a systematic understanding and practical application, it can serve as an instrument of great efficacy in our software development toolkit.

5.1. The Core Concept of Event Sourcing

Event Sourcing revolves around storing all changes made to the application state as a sequence of events. This sequence not only provides the state of the application at any point but also includes an inherent history of how and why it reached that particular state.

In a typical CRUD application, the state is directly manipulated within the database, and these changes are considered the final and absolute state. However, in an event-sourced system, all changes are encapsulated as events and appended to an event log.

5.2. Event Sourcing versus Traditional Approach

Compared with the conventional approach of CRUD operations, Event Sourcing offers a more comprehensive look at the state of an application. But it's not just about recording every intricate detail. The real power of Event Sourcing lies in its capacity to replay these events: to manifest any historical state of the application.

Suppose you've been following traditional practices, where you maintain the current state of an object in the database. In case of any failure or anomaly in the system, determining what led to the mishap can be an arduous task. Here, Event Sourcing comes to the rescue. With this pattern, you possess a log of all the events leading to the mishap.

5.3. Event Store: The Backbone of Event-Sourced Systems

The event store retains all events in an event-sourced system. Unlike conventional databases, the event store is append-only: new events are added to the end, and existing events should never be modified or deleted.

Each event specifies the type of change that occurred along with additional details. Event stores are often implemented with databases capable of handling large amounts of data for their ability to scale and maintain performance.

5.4. Benefits of Event Sourcing

1. Audit Trail: event sourcing provides an audit trail out of the box. Any change made to the system is recorded as an event in a log,

providing comprehensive traceability.

2. Temporal Query: because the state at any point is derived from the event log, it is possible to recreate the state at any specific point in time.

3. Error Diagnosis: the complete history of events helps in tracking down the unlikely behaviors and bugs in the system.

4. Event Replay: the ability to recreate any state of the application by replaying events is a characteristic feature of event sourcing, useful for backups and debugging.

5.5. Roadblocks to Event Sourcing

1. Complexity: event sourcing increases complexity in design and implementation, as the state is not directly managed but derived from a series of events.

2. Event Versioning: once an event is stored in the log, it cannot be amended. This poses a challenge when events need to be updated, requiring some form of versioning strategy.

3. Query Handling: querying in an event-sourced system can be an intricate task as you constantly need to reconstruct the state from the event log.

While these challenges exist, the foremost step towards overcoming them lies in understanding the inherent trade-offs and aligning the choice of this pattern with your specific needs.

5.6. Practical Implementation of Event Sourcing

While understanding the theory of event sourcing is necessary, seeing it applied practically can significantly enhance comprehension. Let's consider a basic event-sourced system with

Order as the aggregate root, capturing various events like `OrderCreated`, `ItemAdded`, `ItemRemoved`, and `OrderCompleted`.

We'll start by defining the `Order` class and its initial state, followed by defining events and using them to alter the state. For each event, a corresponding function is implemented in the `Order` class, which is invoked upon the occurrence of that event.

Building an event-sourced system necessitates a different approach, favoring events over state. It's reminiscent of building a time machine that takes us through multiple points in our application's lifespan.

This chapter has shed light on the fascinating world of Event Sourcing, a key instrument in our software development toolkit. Its transformative potential and robust characteristics position it as an essential method for understanding the state of our system. As with any tool, the key lies in knowing when and how to use it effectively. Despite its complexities, the art of Event Sourcing is one that is worth mastering, due to its ability to provide unprecedented insights into your application's state, past, present, and future.

Chapter 6. Creating Order from Chaos: How Event Sourcing Works

Creating order from chaos often requires a paradigm shift in thinking. With event sourcing, we apply the concept wherein changes to the application state are logged as a sequence of events, opening up a wealth of information but also introducing new challenges. To comprehend how event sourcing works, let's step into its mechanics.

6.1. The Principle Behind Event Sourcing

Event sourcing isn't a new idea by any means. It's modeled around the idea that every change to the state of an application should be captured in an event object. Those objects, when sequenced, describe the state of the application over time.

```java
public class OrderPlacedEvent {

    private final String orderId;
    private final String product;
    private final String customer;

    // Constructors, getters, setters omitted for
brevity
}
```

In the code snippet above, we're modeling an event representing the placement of an order. Each instance of OrderPlacedEvent represents a singular action regarding an order.

6.2. Tracking Applications' State Changes

Most applications prior to the introduction of event sourcing maintained their state in a database, only reflecting the current state and losing the journey of how we arrived at it. With event sourcing, we keep a history of state transactions, providing us with significant leads to trace the state of an application at any given time.

For instance, when an application processed the `OrderPlacedEvent`, rather than just updating the order status to `placed` in a database table, it would record an `OrderPlacedEvent` with the order information. These events are then stored in an extensive log known as the event store. Event stores become the source of truth for our application, encapsulating the system's full history.

Being able to rewind or fast-forward application state becomes a potent tool, equipping us with greater insights, and holds immense value for complex systems.

6.3. Setting up the Event Store

Setting up the event store is one of the crucial parts of this journey. This needs to be resilient, durable, and, most importantly, fast. It should be capable of handling massive amounts of read and write operations without compromise in performance.

Generally, the event store isn't used to serve any business queries; it's only there to record events and playback when required. Event store could be any storage system, in-memory or persistent, based on the nature of your application and consistency requirements.

```
public interface EventStore {

    void saveEvent(OrderPlacedEvent event);

    List<OrderPlacedEvent> getAllEvents();
}
```

Here, we have defined an `EventStore` interface containing methods to save an event and fetch all events.

6.4. Event Playbacks

An extraordinary feature of event sourcing is the ability to replay events. By going through the event log and executing all events, we can recreate the application state at any given point in time. This opens up possibilities for historical debugging, rewinding the state to a known good state in cases of system failure, and more.

An event replay might look something like this:

```
public void replayEvents() {
    List<OrderPlacedEvent> events =
eventStore.getAllEvents();
    for (OrderPlacedEvent event : events) {
        apply(event);
    }
}
```

This method fetches all events from the event store and applies them in the order they were saved.

At first, the freedom and power of event sourcing can seem overwhelming, but with good practices and methods, you can create order from chaos. Event sourcing allows us to track every twist and turn our data went under, granting an overview of the past and improving our vision for the future. It transforms the data from just being a static snapshot to a dynamic narrative of our system's life, providing countless benefits to developers and businesses alike.

Ultimately, Event Sourcing pushes us to view our software systems not as collections of static, unconnected states but as a continuous flow of updates, changes, and developments, turning chaotic randomness into structured, insightful journeys.

Chapter 7. The Synergy of CQRS and Event Sourcing

For many developers, architects, and organizations, the synergy between Command Query Responsibility Segregation (CQRS) and Event Sourcing (ES) constitutes a multifaceted dynamo of modern software architecture. This chapter unpacks the intricate linkages between these two concepts and unravels how their combined application can propel your system design to the vanguard of operational efficiency and resiliency.

7.1. The Intersection of CQRS and Event Sourcing

CQRS and Event Sourcing signal two distinct patterns. While CQRS focuses on the separation of command and query responsibilities, Event Sourcing, in contrast, is concerned with storing changes to an application's state as a sequence of events.

However, their intersection presents a pivotal advantage: With Event Sourcing providing an audit log of changes, it avails a fountain of insightful data that can be leveraged to create numerous read models using the command model. As a result, the system remains faithful to the CQRS principle of keeping writes separate from reads while simultaneously benefiting from the rich record-keeping of the event-driven paradigm.

7.2. Leveraging CQRS to Enhance Event Sourcing

Before we proceed, let's quickly review the mechanics of CQRS. CQRS dictates that modification operations (commands) and retrieval operations (queries) should live in different models. By segregating these responsibilities, your system acquires a degree of flexibility to independently optimize read and write sides to suit specific requirements.

Implementing CQRS with Event Sourcing means event handlers can be utilized to update the read model upon an event's occurrence. The substantial upside here is that alterations to the reading model (say a schema change) need not affect the command models and events since events are solely transformed into projections. This provides the capability to independently evolve read and write models.

7.3. The Perks of an Event-Sourced Command Model

Event Sourcing elevates the effectiveness of the command model by storing every state change as an event. No longer does your system lose valuable context when alterations occur—the 'what', 'why' and 'when' of each change is faithfully recorded.

This approach reintroduces an essential temporal dimension that traditional persistence mechanisms often disregard. An event-sourced command model matches real-world scenarios more accurately, endowing your system with a higher degree of fidelity and enhanced decision-making capabilities.

7.4. Exploiting Event Sourcing for Nascent Read Models

A commonly underestimated advantage of merging CQRS and ES is the ability to construct new read models from pre-existing event data. Such an approach can be a game-changer when requirements change, and new views are needed.

Once a new read model is introduced, it's processed back in time, starting with the first event—effectively getting a full reconstruction of historical events. This doesn't only enable the provision of the new data representation but also ensures its accuracy reflecting past activities.

7.5. Concluding Remarks

As we delved into the unique landscape crafted by the amalgamation of CQRS and ES, it's apparent they have a synergetic relationship. Without Event Sourcing, CQRS could struggle with auditing and historical data while, without CQRS, Event Sourcing could buckle under the weight of its event log.

The amalgam of the two approaches takes advantage of their strengths and shields against their respective weaknesses. Their marriage begets an architecture that embodies flexibility, robustness, and traceability—core characteristics sought by developers when designing intricate and high-performing systems. Understanding the synergy between these two architectural gems is an enriching experience that forms a cornerstone of modern software design. The journey may seem challenging, but it's worth traversing for those who seek to harness their combined power in software applications.

Thus, the chapter concludes on the note that CQRS and ES together make a potent recipe for creating highly efficient, scalable, resilient, and adaptive system architectures.

Chapter 8. Case Studies: Real-world Applications of CQRS and Event Sourcing

When it comes to practical applications of Command Query Responsibility Segregation (CQRS) and Event Sourcing, countless examples manifest in the real world as enterprises of all sizes harness their capabilities. Let's dive deeper into a few explicit cases that reveal how these patterns optimally function in various scenarios.

8.1. Leveraging CQRS in an E-Commerce Application

Consider an e-commerce platform comprising numerous services rendered and a massive volume of orders processed daily. The operations in such a platform may be segregated into two broad categories: Commands (managing products, placing orders) and Queries (browsing products, checking order status).

Using traditional CRUD operations in this setting can lead to inefficiencies due to the disparity between read and write operations' demand and nature. A more effective approach would be to separate them, and this is where CQRS comes into play.

Splitting the application into read-centric and write-centric models helps optimize the operations. While the write portion handles tasks like order placement, the read side takes care of user-facing operations like product searches. To ensure data consistency and eventual synchronicity between these models, events are propagated from the write side to the read side, updating the read model and reflecting changes accurately to the user.

8.2. Event Sourcing in the Financial Industry

Financial transactions inherently possess the property of immutability: once completed, they cannot be altered or deleted. This characteristic aligns perfectly with Event Sourcing's operational mechanics, making it a favorite pattern in the financial sector.

Consider a banking application where all transactions are logged as a series of events. Each account's state change is captured as an event (e.g., account creation, deposit, withdrawal, etc.). Instead of updating the current balance in a conventional data row, Event Sourcing enables us to determine it by playing back the sequence of events associated with the account. Similarly, generating account statements or understanding transaction sequences becomes significantly more straightforward with relevant events for reference.

Aside from these benefits, Event Sourcing also offers an excellent solution for maintaining audit trails and facilitating debugging, immensely useful in the banking domain.

8.3. Using CQRS and Event Sourcing in Microservice Architectures

With the rise of microservices, CQRS and Event Sourcing have found considerable adoption. In a microservices architecture where multiple independent services interact, one service's internal operations shouldn't impact others. Such decoupling is particularly enabled by CQRS; the segregation of command and query responsibilities ensures one service's writes do not inflict undue stress on another service's reads.

Event Sourcing also plays an essential role by providing a powerful means for inter-service communication and maintaining application state across services. Rather than directly querying another service for data, services can instead subscribe to the events that interest them. By persistently storing all state transitions as events, we can recreate the state of any entity at any point, allowing for system-wide state consistency and real-time data replication.

8.4. CQRS and Event Sourcing in IoT Applications

Internet of Things (IoT) presents yet another promising prospect for these patterns. Consider a smart home application where multiple devices are interconnected—each device carries out operations (commands) and reports status (queries).

With the sheer volume of data generated and processed, a traditional CRUD approach can quickly overwhelm the system. Alternately, a CQRS approach can help efficiently manage this data, with commands driving the state change and queries presenting the latest state to the users.

Simultaneously, Event Sourcing can chronologically record these state changes as events. If a user wants to revisit a device's operation pattern a week ago or a month ago, it's achievable by replaying the relevant events.

This exploration of real-world applications provides a glimpse into the transformative potential of CQRS and Event Sourcing. These design patterns can significantly streamline operations in various contexts, confirm a system's robustness, and ensure the scalability of applications. Understanding how to utilize them best in your projects is the first step to harness their full potential.

Chapter 9. Overcoming Challenges: Pitfalls and Solutions in Implementing CQRS & Event Sourcing

The implementation of Command Query Responsibility Segregation (CQRS) and Event Sourcing proves to be powerful, but it does not come without its own set of intricate challenges. By understanding these pitfalls and making informed decisions to overcome these obstacles, you can expect to put these principles into practice effectively and efficiently.

9.1. Understanding the Challenges

Know that the implementation of CQRS and Event Sourcing is not a linear, textbook process. It is rather a nuanced and arduous journey that provides the participants ample opportunities to learn. With its deep, transformative impact on system architecture, several obstacles must be tackled.

It is vital to recognize that CQRS and Event Sourcing are not a one-size-fits-all solution. For some use cases, these patterns may be overkill, leading to unnecessary complexity. Some common challenges with implementation include complexity in data handling, necessary commitment to automated testing, difficulties with data versioning, and maintaining data consistency.

9.2. Complexity in Data Handling

Owing to its dual model approach, CQRS inherently places a burden of extra complexity on the system. Handling commands and queries separately can lead to an increase in code complexity because you are essentially maintaining two data models.

In the context of event sourcing, data is stored as a sequence of events rather than a single state. This approach can lead to an increase in system complexity as you must maintain and manage event logs which can grow large over time. Furthermore, without careful design and planning, replaying events can potentially be a time-consuming operation.

To mitigate these potential issues, consider the following:

Implement a layer of abstraction to isolate the complexity to a specific area of the codebase. This would aid in maintaining the sanity of the codebase and improve maintainability.

Establish strategies for managing event logs, including their archival and deletion after a certain period.

If event sourcing brings too much complexity, have a backup plan where you can drop back to traditional CRUD operations with minimum modification.

9.3. A Commitment to Automated Testing

With CQRS and Event Sourced systems, the need for extensive automated testing is inevitable. Given the asynchronous nature and the distributed architecture of such systems, manual testing can be time-consuming and often misses edge scenarios.

Moreover, in event sourcing, the state of the application is derived from the sequence of past events. Figuring out bugs in the system might require you to evaluate logs of historical events, proving to be a tedious task.

To overcome these challenges:

Make automated testing a built-in part of your system development. This should extend beyond just unit testing to encompass functional, integration, and end-to-end testing.

Use advanced logging and monitoring systems to trace any anomaly in the system back to the right event.

9.4. Dealing with Data Versioning

This is a complex problem related to Event Sourcing. Events in an event-sourced system are immutable. Once an event is recorded, it can't be changed. This characteristic throws a challenge: What happens when the historic events are recorded in a format that needs to be changed?

To handle these issues:

Events should be versioned to ensure the system can handle new event formats. All new events should be assigned a current version number.

If historical events need to be changed, it is recommended to use upcasting, which allows to convert

the older versions of the event to the newer ones on the
fly.

9.5. Maintaining Data Consistency

Maintaining consistency is the primary challenge with the
implementation of CQRS. The practice of keeping separate models for
command and query can lead to eventual consistency, which implies
that there might be a slight delay in reflecting command operations
in the query model.

In order to handle eventual consistency:

Implement strategies of eventual consistency like read
or write quorums, or compensating transactions. This
will ensure that your system is consistent over a
period, if not immediately.

Use Domain-Driven Design (DDD) to focus and handle
specific business use cases where immediate consistency
is required.

While the journey of implementing CQRS and Event Sourcing is
challenging, it also provides a great learning opportunity. A keen
understanding and effective management of these challenges help in
harnessing the true power of these patterns in an applications life-
cycle. By creating thoughtful solutions to these potential problems,
teams can take steps to create resilient, scalable, and highly
functional systems.

Chapter 10. Futuristic View: The Evolving Landscape of CQRS and Event Sourcing

In the current software development landscape, there's been a significant shift towards building systems that are distributed, have the ability to scale, and can handle significant amounts of data. It's in this evolving landscape that CQRS (Command Query Responsibility Segregation) and Event Sourcing come into play and continuously blaze new trails.

10.1. The Emergence of Distributed Systems

Distributed systems grant a considerable degree of robustness and availability to applications. These systems, by their nature, consist of various services operating concurrently, often communicating via a network, aiming to achieve a common goal. This design facilitates growth, allowing for services to respond independently to increasing demands.

CQRS and Event Sourcing come to the fore in such settings. With CQRS, the complexity of the system is reduced by separating the write operations (commands) and read operations (queries), each having different models. Meanwhile, Event Sourcing introduces an alternative approach of storing state changes as events, allowing the construction of the system's elapse chronologically.

10.2. Eventual Consistency and CQRS

In distributed systems, synchronizing the state of every microservice or every database in real-time is an expensive, often unwieldy task. Instead, developers often lean towards an 'eventual consistency' model, making CQRS an optimal fit.

CQRS doesn't insist on instantaneous consistency. Instead, after issuing a command, the client must be patient until the view model is updated. Here, CQRS shines as it can handle the asynchronicity optimally, with segregated command-query operations, leading to applications that are more resilient and adaptive.

10.3. Event-Driven Architectures and Event Sourcing

Distributed systems, especially with microservices, are evolving to adopt event-driven architectures. In such cases, operations are responses to the occurrence of specific events, creating a more fluid, responsive system.

Event Sourcing fits like a glove in such environments. Instead of focussing on the current state, it enables us to capture all changes to an application's state as an ordered sequence of events.

Any 'state' can then be derived from the replay of these events. And given the granular nature of data stored, this pattern brilliantly caters to auditing requirements, debugging, and system behavior understanding.

10.4. The Role of CQRS and Event Sourcing in IoT

The Internet of Things (IoT) stands at the frontier of technology, producing an enormous volume of data. Handling such data and making quick decisions based on it forms a considerable challenge.

CQRS, with its segregation of command and query operations, allows IoT systems to efficiently handle massive amounts of data by scaling these two operations independently. Event Sourcing, on the other hand, empowers IoT systems to audit and trace data, an important feature given the importance and sensitivity of data flowing within such ecosystems.

10.5. Real-Time Applications and the Influence of CQRS

In applications that demand real-time or near-real-time updates, CQRS has shown its mettle. The pattern's segregation feature also extends to the models used to write to and read from databases, allowing them to be optimized to better handle their intended operations. This, in turn, gives real-time applications more flexibility, especially concerning database schema and query optimization.

10.6. The Impact of CQRS and Event Sourcing on Performance Optimization

The efficient scaling of operations independently and concurrent operation execution that CQRS offers can significantly influence a system's performance. Similarly, Event Sourcing offers unique performance optimizations—the event store is append-only, giving a performance benefit for write-intensive applications.

In conclusion, CQRS and Event Sourcing, as potent tools for an evolving software landscape, are not merely patterns to implement on a whim. They entail a considerable learning curve and bring a degree of complexity. However, they offer undeniable robustness, scalability, and flexibility in return. Therefore, as paradigms shift towards distributed, real-time, event-driven, and IoT-based systems, the relevance of mastering CQRS and Event Sourcing becomes even more pronounced.

Chapter 11. Embarking the Journey: Project Practicals with CQRS and Event Sourcing

Kickstarting our expedition, let's delve into some hands-on experience of implementing CQRS and Event Sourcing in a real-world project. Our goal here is not merely to explain these concepts in pure theoretical terms but also to connect them with practical scenarios, making the learning process more significant and impactful.

11.1. Initiation: Understanding the Basics

Before starting the project's actual implementation, we need to understand the basics of CQRS (Command Query Responsibility Segregation) and Event Sourcing.

CQRS is simply a design pattern that separates the write and read operations of a system into two distinct models, enhancing system performance while providing a more robust solution. For developers who manage hefty data-driven applications, CQRS provides a lifeline to tackle complexity.

Event Sourcing, on the other hand, is a technique that eschews traditional data storage models. Instead of storing its current state, an application utilizing Event Sourcing stores the series of domain events leading to the current situation. This unconventional approach provides incredible benefits, including richer business insights, reliable audit logs, and superior system behavior understanding.

11.2. Constructing a Domain Model

Time to move from theory to action! Our first task is to construct a domain model for our application by identifying the significant components that interact with our system.

In asciidoc markup, a typical domain model might look something like this:

```
[options="header"]
|===
| Component | Description
| User | Represents the person using the software
product
| System | Represents the CQRS/Event-Sourced application
we're developing
| Product | Represents the object being sold
| Payment | Represents the transaction made by the User
|===
```

Every component in the domain model will have read and write services, with each carrying out a distinct set of responsibilities.

11.3. Implementing CQRS

With our domain model ready, let's proceed to implement CQRS. Our focus would involve segregating the read and write operations for each component, ensuring that each operation adheres to a distinct service.

Here's what the pseudocode for our segregated system might look like:

```
[options="header"]
```

```
|===
| Component | Command (Write) Operations | Query (Read)
Operations
| User | Register, Log In, Change Password | Retrieve
Profile, Retrieve Purchase History
| System | Process Transactions, Generate Reports |
Retrieve User Info, Retrieve Product Info, Retrieve
Transaction History
| Product | Add, Update, Remove | Retrieve All, Retrieve
Single
| Payment | Make Payment, Refund | Retrieve Transaction
Details, Retrieve Refund Status
|===
```

11.4. Applying Event Sourcing

Now that we've successfully implemented CQRS, let's build upon it by incorporating event sourcing. Every state change event will now be recorded, offering us a near-perfect system audit log, an excellent resource for debugging and system state recreation, and facilitating robust business insights.

Implementing Event Sourcing typically involves introducing event store and event handler components into the system.

The event store is where the events get recorded. It's essentially a database storage system but designed specifically for handling events. On the other hand, the event handler processes the events from the event store, is responsible for updating the query model, and can trigger other operations based on the events.

11.5. Pacing Together CQRS and Event Sourcing

After building up our application with CQRS and Event Sourcing respectively, it's time for the pivotal moment - bringing everything together. The integrated system will get us the best of both worlds. This interplay will transcend the usual CRUD-based programming, allowing us to cater to complex business needs and requirements with greater ease.

Wrapping up, studying CQRS and Event Sourcing is a thrilling journey, rather like ascending a mountain peak while discovering new landscapes. As you embrace these design patterns, it's critical to explore them both theoretically and practically, sharpening your understanding and application of each. The final vista is undeniably worth the trek - a robust, scalable, and insight-rich application promising enriched user experiences and business benefits. Happy Coding!